ZPL

# Bot Maker

# BUILD YOUR OWN

# BUG BOT

## Tucker Besel

BLACK
RABBIT
BOOKS

Hi Jinx is published by Black Rabbit Books
P.O. Box 3263, Mankato, Minnesota, 56002.
www.blackrabbitbooks.com
Copyright © 2018 Black Rabbit Books

Jennifer Besel, editor; Michael Sellner, designer;
Catherine Cates, production designer;
Omay Ayres, photo researcher

Library of Congress Cataloging-in-Publication Data
Names: Besel, Tucker, author.
Title: Build your own bug bot /
by Tucker Besel.
Description: Mankato, Minnesota :
Black Rabbit Books, [2018] | Series: Hi jinx.
Bot maker | Audience: Age 9-12. | Audience:
Grade 4 to 6. | Includes bibliographical
references and index.
Identifiers: LCCN 2017007096 (print) |
LCCN 2017037519 (ebook) | ISBN 9781680723519
(eBook) | ISBN 9781680723212 (library binding) |
ISBN 9781680726459 (paperback)
Subjects: LCSH: Robots—Design and construction—Juvenile
literature. | Robotic pets—Juvenile literature.
Classification: LCC TJ211.2 (ebook) | LCC TJ211.2 .B484 2018
(print) | DDC 629.8/932—dc23
LC record available at https://lccn.loc.gov/2017007096

Printed in the United States. 10/17

## Image Credits

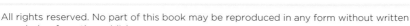

Grant Gould, all robot illustrations
Alamy: age fotostock, 20 (l); DEFENSE ADVANCED RESEARCH PROJECTS
AGENCY: http://www.darpa.mil/, 20 (r); Dreamstime: Ect100, 5 (pipe
cleaner); Karen Hoar, 5 (eyes); Simm49, 5 (aligator clip); iStock:
mediaphotos, 4 (kids); Shutterstock: advent, 19 (kid); Arcady, 8
(note); Art'nLera, 3, 12, 21 (bkgd); belka_35, 5 (scissors); Big
Boy, 17 (bug); Bplanet, 5 (motor); Dualororua, 13 (hands);
Fedorov Oleksiy, 5 (pencil); Galyna G, 1, 5, 7, 8, 11, 15, 18-19
(bkgd); GraphicsRF, 5 (clips); GreenStockCreative, 5 (eraser);
hoomoo, 5 (pliers); iceink, 5, 7 (glue gun); Jumnong, 5
(tape); Muhammad Desta Laksana, 16 (spider); niwat
chaiyawoot, 11 (pliers); opicobello, 16 (scribble); Pasko
Maksim, 14, 18, 23, 24 (torn paper); PILart, 7 (glue); Pitju,
3, 21 (curled paper); Pixel Embargo, 6, 15 (pencil); restyler,
5, 10 (battery); Roberto Castillo, Cover (bkgd); Rohit
Dhanaji Shinde, 16 (chameleon); Rohit Dhanaji Shinde,
3 (ant); 6, 15, 19 (ant), 24 (ant); ScofieldZa, 5 (ruler);
SeneGal, 14 (dog); shockfactor.de, 16 (fly); tankist276,
5 (glasses); Teguh Mujiono, 8, 11, 12, 21 (bug); Thomas
Bethge, 5 (sticks); totallypic, 8-9, 10-11, 12-13, 14-15
(arrows); Tueris, Cover, 1, 3, 4, 6, 9, 20 (marker stains);
umnola, 1 (ant); Vidux, 6-7 (ruler); Winai Tepsuttinun,
5, 10 (battery pack); your, 16 (clouds) Every effort has
been made to contact copyright holders for material
reproduced in this book. Any omissions will be rectified in
subsequent printings if notice is given to the publisher.

# CONTENTS

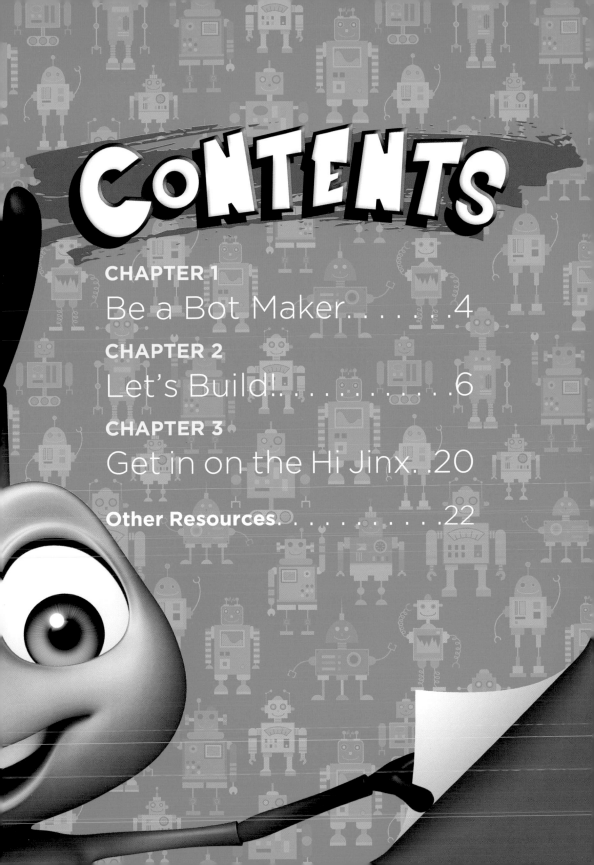

**CHAPTER 1**

Be a Bot Maker........4

**CHAPTER 2**

Let's Build!..............6

**CHAPTER 3**

Get in on the Hi Jinx..20

**Other Resources**...........22

# Chapter 1

BE A BOT MAKER

Robots aren't just for movies. People are creating robots that walk, run, and battle. Even beginners can create bots that wiggle and roll.

This book will help you create your own simple bug robot. Robot building takes patience. Don't give up if something isn't working. Experiment until it does. And, most importantly, have fun!

# WHAT YOU'LL NEED

ruler

sharpened pencil

5 4½-inch- (11-cm-)
long popsicle sticks

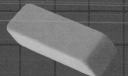
3 1-inch- (2.5-cm-)
long paper clips

large eraser

scissors

googly eyes

pipe cleaners

2 AA batteries

pliers

1¼-inch (3-cm)
alligator clip

enclosed AA battery pack
that holds two batteries (with
½ inch [1 cm] of wire exposed)

6-volt toy motor with wires
(with ½ inch [1 cm]
of wire exposed)

electrical tape

safety glasses

hot glue gun
and hot glue

# Chapter 2

# LET'S BUILD!

1. Use the ruler to mark a popsicle stick at 1½ inches (4 cm) from one end. Make another mark at 3 inches (8 cm). Break the stick at the marks. You should have three **equal** pieces.

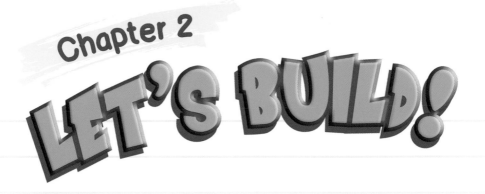

3 inches →

1 ½ inches →

left side

Lay the other four popsicle sticks side by side on your workspace. Hot glue one short piece across the center of the four long sticks. Glue one short piece across the left side. Then glue the last short piece across the right side.

**3.** Straighten one paper clip. Measure 1 inch (2.5 cm) from the end. At that spot, bend the clip to make an "L." Repeat this on the other end of the clip. When done, it should look like a wide "U."

**4.** Repeat step 3 with the other paper clips.

Did you know all insects have six legs? Well, now you know.

front of bot

**5.** Hot glue the paper clips to the short sticks to make legs. On the side pieces, glue the clips to the inside edges. In the middle, glue a clip to either side of the short stick. The side the clip is closer to is the front of your bot.

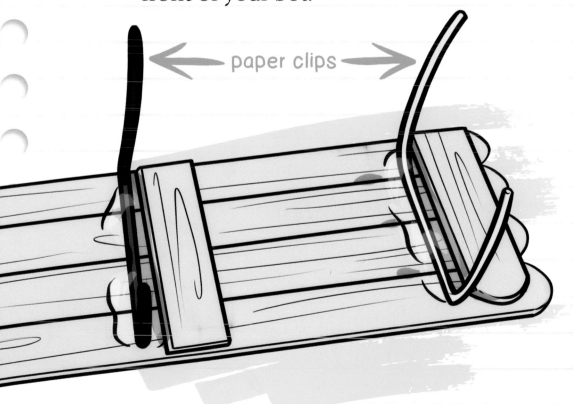

paper clips

**6.** Flip the bot over so it's "standing" on the legs. Bend the clips as needed to make them all touch the ground.

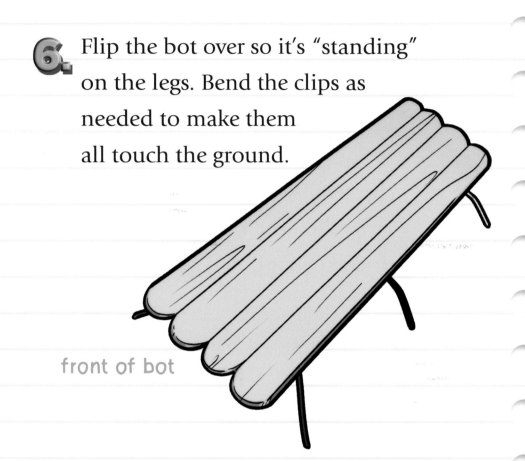

front of bot

**7.** Put the batteries in the battery pack. If there's a power switch, turn it on.

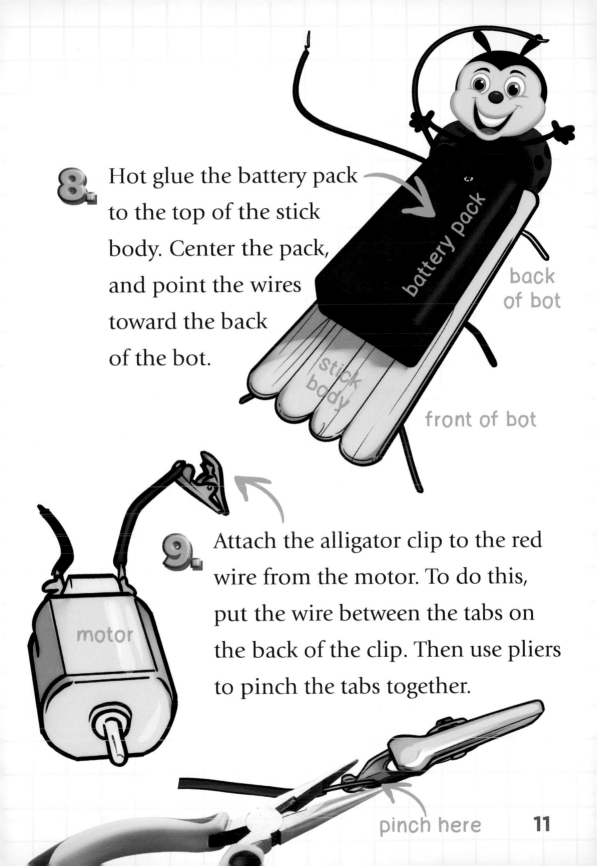

**8.** Hot glue the battery pack to the top of the stick body. Center the pack, and point the wires toward the back of the bot.

battery pack

back of bot

stick body

front of bot

**9.** Attach the alligator clip to the red wire from the motor. To do this, put the wire between the tabs on the back of the clip. Then use pliers to pinch the tabs together.

motor

pinch here

11

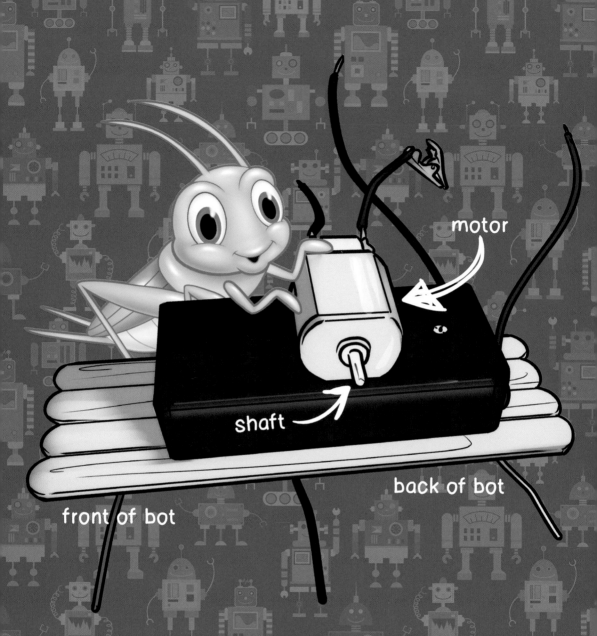

motor

shaft

back of bot

front of bot

**10.** Hot glue the motor to the top center of the battery pack. Make sure the **shaft** sticks out past the "body."

**11.** Connect the black wires from the battery pack and motor. To do that, hold the exposed parts of the black wires side by side. Then twist them together. **Clamp** the alligator clip to the battery pack's exposed red wire. The motor's shaft should spin. Then unclamp the clip.

**12.** Bend the twisted wire ends down. Wrap them to the black wire with electrical tape.

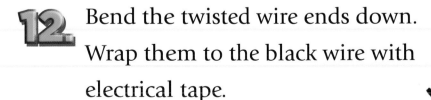

**13.** Clean up the wires. Fold them together and hot glue them to the battery pack. Make sure the alligator clip can reach the exposed red wire.

glued to battery pack

front of bot

**14.** Cut a ½-inch (1-cm) cube from the eraser. Use a pencil to poke a hole in the eraser. The hole should be a little off-center.

½ inch

½ inch

off-center

**15.** Press the motor's shaft into the hole. Hot glue the eraser to the shaft.

front of bot

**16.** Make your robot look like an insect. Hot glue eyes to the front side of the battery pack.

**17.** Bend pipe cleaners to look like **antennae**. Hot glue them to the top of the battery pack.

**18.** Glue on whatever other decorations you wish.

**19.** Finally, make the insect "walk." Clamp the alligator clip to the exposed red wire. The insect should **vibrate** and scurry across the table!

# Chapter 3
# GET IN ON THE HI JINX

Robot scientists are doing amazing things. Medical robots save people's lives. Animal robots might one day help soldiers in battle. Now you have the skills to create your own robots. How will you change the world?

# Take It One Step More

1. What happens if you bend the legs of your bot differently?

2. What role does the eraser play in this bot?

3. How could you build on this design? Is there a way to make this robot start and stop on its own?

# GLOSSARY

**antenna** (ahn-TEN-uh)—one of a pair of skinny organs on the heads of insects

**clamp** (KLAMP)—to hold tightly

**equal** (EE-kwuhl)—the same measure, quantity, or amount as another

**exposed** (ek-SPOZD)—not covered

**shaft** (SHAFT)—a cylindrical bar used to support rotating pieces

**vibrate** (VI-brayt)—to swing or move to and fro

## BOOKS

**Cunningham, Kevin.** *Robot Scientist.* Cool STEAM Careers. Ann Arbor, MI: Cherry Lake Publishing, 2016.

**Derrington, Louise.** *How to Build Robots.* Technology in Motion. New York: Crabtree Publishing Company, 2017.

**McCombs, Kevin.** *Locomotion and Mechanics.* Robotics. New York: Cavendish Square Publishing, 2017.

## WEBSITES

Build Your First Robot
**www.popularmechanics.com/technology/robots/a7388/build-your-first-robot/**

History of Robotics: Timeline
**www.robotshop.com/media/files/PDF/timeline.pdf**

Robotics: Facts
**idahoptv.org/sciencetrek/topics/robots/facts.cfm**

Adults are boring. But they can be really helpful. Don't be afraid to ask for help if you get stuck.

If your wires don't have exposed ends, don't worry. Use a wire stripper to take off as much of the wire casing as needed. (See first tip.)

Try using different sizes of eraser to see which one works best. You could also try using a different material, such as cork.

The author is super cool. He made a short video of his bug bot. Check it out on Black Rabbit Books' YouTube channel.

8/18